MARTIAL ARTS

MUAY THAI

BY JULIANNA HELT

WWW.APEXEDITIONS.COM

Copyright © 2024 by Apex Editions, Mendota Heights, MN 55120. All rights reserved. No part of this book may be reproduced or utilized in any form or by any means without written permission from the publisher.

Apex is distributed by North Star Editions:
sales@northstareditions.com | 888-417-0195

Produced for Apex by Red Line Editorial.

Photographs ©: Peerapon Boonyakiat/SOPA Images/Sipa USA/AP Images, cover; Shutterstock Images, 1, 4–5, 6, 7, 8, 12, 13, 14, 15, 16–17, 18, 19, 20–21, 22–23, 24–25, 26, 27, 29; Chris Hellier/Alamy, 10–11

Library of Congress Control Number: 2023910148

ISBN
978-1-63738-767-2 (hardcover)
978-1-63738-810-5 (paperback)
978-1-63738-892-1 (ebook pdf)
978-1-63738-853-2 (hosted ebook)

Printed in the United States of America
Mankato, MN
012024

NOTE TO PARENTS AND EDUCATORS

Apex books are designed to build literacy skills in striving readers. Exciting, high-interest content attracts and holds readers' attention. The text is carefully leveled to allow students to achieve success quickly. Additional features, such as bolded glossary words for difficult terms, help build comprehension.

TABLE OF CONTENTS

CHAPTER 1
MUAY THAI FIGHTERS 4

CHAPTER 2
A LONG HISTORY 10

CHAPTER 3
MANY MOVES 16

CHAPTER 4
MUAY THAI TODAY 22

COMPREHENSION QUESTIONS • 28
GLOSSARY • 30
TO LEARN MORE • 31
ABOUT THE AUTHOR • 31
INDEX • 32

CHAPTER 1

MUAY THAI FIGHTERS

A Muay Thai **bout** is about to begin. Two fighters enter the ring. They wear padded gloves and headgear.

4

The headgear fighters wear during Muay Thai is called a Mongkhon.

Fighters bow to show respect for their parents and teachers.

The fighters perform a **ritual**. First, they walk around the ring. They say prayers. Next, they bow. After that, they do a dance.

TIES TO TRADITION

Sarama plays during bouts. It is **traditional** music from Thailand. It uses drums and cymbals. Each fighter also wears a traditional armband. It is said to give luck.

Armbands are called Pra Jiads. Traditionally, they are pieces of a fighter's mother's clothing.

Then the fight begins. The fighters kick, punch, and jab. One fighter knocks out his opponent. He wins the bout.

FAST FACT
There are usually five rounds in each Muay Thai bout. Each round lasts three minutes.

◀ Muay Thai is similar to boxing. But fighters can strike with both their arms and their legs.

CHAPTER 2

A LONG HISTORY

Muay Thai comes from the **Siamese** army. In the 1200s, its soldiers created a style of hand-to-hand fighting.

Before 1939, Thailand was known as Siam.

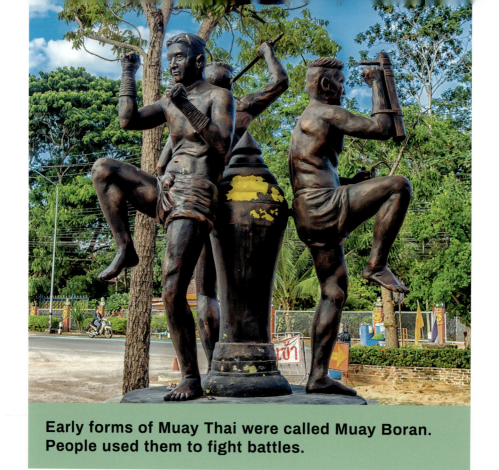

Early forms of Muay Thai were called Muay Boran. People used them to fight battles.

By the 1600s, this style developed into Muay Thai. People used it to defend their land. It became Thailand's national sport. Many towns held **tournaments**.

IN DISGUISE

King Prachao Sua lived from 1662 to 1709. He loved to **compete** in Muay Thai. But he always wore a **disguise**. That way, no one would know they were fighting the king.

Many cities in Thailand still hold tournaments. They often take place in stadiums.

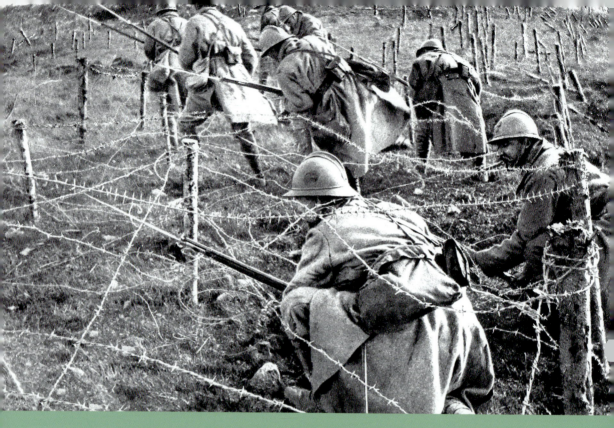

Many battles took place in France during World War I (1914–1918). Thai soldiers fought in some of them.

In the 1900s, Thai soldiers fought in France. They taught people there Muay Thai. Muay Thai spread to other countries as well. Events began taking place all over the world.

FAST FACT
At first, only men were allowed to do Muay Thai. Later, women could compete, too.

Today, many countries host men's and women's Muay Thai events.

CHAPTER 3

MANY MOVES

Muay Thai is sometimes called "the art of eight limbs." Fighters use their fists, knees, elbows, and shins.

Muay Thai is one of the only martial arts that allows hits with knees and elbows.

In a clinch, a fighter's arms wrap around the other person's neck or shoulders.

Fighters practice many types of kicks and punches. They also learn how to clinch. To clinch, fighters grab each other's arms and head. This helps them prepare to attack.

ROUNDHOUSE KICKS

Roundhouse kicks are the hardest and strongest moves in Muay Thai. Fighters swing their legs from the hip. They hit **opponents** with their shins. The swinging movement provides lots of power.

A roundhouse kick to the face can knock out an opponent.

Several attacks use the knees. Some moves jab at an opponent's chest or thighs. Other moves target the face. These moves cause lots of damage.

FAST FACT

In flying knee strikes, fighters jump into the air.

CHAPTER 4

Muay Thai Today

To study Muay Thai, people often take classes at gyms. They use hanging bags to practice kicks and strikes. Thick gloves protect their hands.

Bags help fighters practice doing many kicks and punches in a row.

Some fighters go to events. The events divide fighters by gender and weight. People are paired up to fight bouts. Each bout is split into rounds.

FAST FACT
A Nak Muay is a male Muay Thai fighter. A female fighter is called a Muay Ying.

Muay Thai bouts can draw large crowds.

Judges watch. They give fighters points for each round. The fighter with the highest score wins the bout. Fighters can also win by knocking out opponents.

Each round's winner gets 10 points. The other fighter gets fewer points.

People in Thailand practice several traditional fighting styles. Each focuses on different moves.

FORBIDDEN MOVES

Muay Thai can be violent. But certain moves are not allowed. Hitting eyes or **joints** is forbidden. So are strikes to the back of the head.

COMPREHENSION QUESTIONS

Write your answers on a separate piece of paper.

1. Write a few sentences describing when and where Muay Thai first began.

2. Would you rather be a judge or a fighter in a Muay Thai bout? Why?

3. Which part of the ritual before a Muay Thai bout happens first?
    - **A.** praying
    - **B.** bowing
    - **C.** dancing

4. What are the eight limbs used in Muay Thai?
    - **A.** the weapons that fighters hold
    - **B.** the fists, feet, legs, head, and neck of each fighter
    - **C.** the two fists, two elbows, two knees, and two shins of each fighter

5. What does **target** mean in this book?

*Several attacks use the knees. Some moves jab at an opponent's chest or thighs. Other moves **target** the face.*

   A. run from
   B. aim at
   C. take away

6. What does **forbidden** mean in this book?

*But certain moves are not allowed. Hitting eyes or joints is **forbidden**.*

   A. hard to learn
   B. against the rules
   C. fine to do

Answer key on page 32.

GLOSSARY

bout
One fight that is split into several rounds.

compete
To try to beat others in a game or event.

disguise
Clothes that hide who someone is.

joints
Parts of the body where bones connect, such as the knees.

opponents
People that someone is fighting against.

ritual
A series of actions that have religious meaning.

Siamese
Coming from Siam, a kingdom in Asia that later became the country of Thailand.

tournaments
Events where people try to win several matches or rounds.

traditional
Using ideas or ways of doing things that began long ago.

TO LEARN MORE

BOOKS

Corso, Phil. *Jujitsu*. New York: PowerKids Press, 2020.

Krohn, Frazer Andrew. *MMA: Heroic History*. Minneapolis: Abdo Publishing, 2023.

Osborne, M. K. *Combat Sports*. Mankato, MN: Amicus, 2020.

ONLINE RESOURCES

Visit **www.apexeditions.com** to find links and resources related to this title.

ABOUT THE AUTHOR

Julianna Helt is a former children's librarian turned children's book author. She enjoys researching and writing about all sorts of topics. She lives in Pittsburgh with her husband, two teenagers, and three cats.

INDEX

A
armband, 7

C
clinch, 18

G
gloves, 4, 22

H
headgear, 4,

K
kicks, 9, 18–19, 22
knees, 16, 20

M
Muay Ying, 25

N
Nak Muay, 25

P
Prachao Sua, 13
punches, 9, 18

R
ritual, 6
rounds, 9, 24, 26

S
Sarama, 7
Siamese army, 10

T
Thailand, 7, 12
tournaments, 12

ANSWER KEY:
1. Answers will vary; 2. Answers will vary; 3. A; 4. C; 5. B; 6. B